THE G.I. SERIES

Left: In 1858 a new hat of fur felt was to be looped on the left side for enlisted foot soldiers and on the right side for mounted troops and all officers, although considerable variation existed. Company-grade officers (second lieutenants through captains) were to have two black ostrich feathers on the left side and a gold embroidered branch insignia on the front, in this case crossed cannons for artillery. This officer's dark blue trousers display an ⅛-inch scarlet welt, the branch color for artillery, let into the outer seams. This was the typical uniform of regular army company-grade officers at the outset of the Civil War. *RB*

THE G.I. SERIES

THE ILLUSTRATED HISTORY OF THE AMERICAN SOLDIER, HIS UNIFORM AND HIS EQUIPMENT

Terrible Swift Sword

Union Artillery, Cavalry and Infantry, 1861–1865

John P. Langellier

CHELSEA HOUSE PUBLISHERS
Philadelphia

First Chelsea House hardback edition published 2002.

Designed by David Gibbons, DAG Publications Ltd
Layout by Anthony A. Evans, DAG Publications Ltd
Edited by Wendy Pillar

Printed in China

Library of Congress Cataloging-in-Publication Data
(on file)

DEDICATION
This book is dedicated to Dr. Michael J. McAfee for his unselfish assistance to many students of the American Civil War.

ACKNOWLEDGEMENTS AND ABBREVIATIONS
The author wishes to thank the individuals and staffs of the institutions noted below:

GNMP	Gettysburg National Military Park, Gettysburg, PA
KSHS	Kansas State Historical Society, Topeka
LC	Library of Congress, Washington, DC
MJM	Dr. Michael J. McAfee
NA	National Archives, Still Photography Division, College Park, MD
RB	Robert G. Borrell, Sr
USAMHI	U.S. Army Military History Institute, Carlisle Barracks, PA
USAQM	U.S. Army Quartermaster Museum, Ft Lee, VA
WCC	Western Costume Company, North Hollywood, CA

TERRIBLE SWIFT SWORD: UNION ARTILLERY, CAVALRY AND INFANTRY, 1861–1865

The Civil War in some respects might be viewed as the end of warfare as it had been known in the eighteenth and nineteenth centuries and the beginning of modern 'total war'. On 12 April 1861, when the war exploded with the firing on Fort Sumter, South Carolina by 'rebel' forces, the regular army of the United States Army counted only 15,304 enlisted men and 1098 officers. By the conflict's end, in April 1865, that number had swollen to nearly a million men – the lion's share of whom were volunteers.

Over the years the soldiers fighting for the Union came to be viewed popularly as blue-clad fighters who faced Confederates in gray and butternut. In reality, the color of the uniforms varied on both sides, as did weapons, tactics and accouterments. In fact, after Fort Sumter Union militiamen and volunteers reported in a wide variety of uniforms. Some set off in civilian clothing, being distinguished as soldiers only by their weapons and accouterments. Others found simple, gray outfits ample. Several adopted more elaborate European-inspired costumes such as French zouave-like garb, towering Napoleonic bearskins, British havelocks (named after the English officer, whose distinguished service in India just a few years earlier had popularized the device), feathered Italian *bersaglieri* headgear, Scottish kilts and tartan trews, and green ensembles for Irish American groups (and eventually for sharpshooters).

Even regulars presented a mixed appearance, such as the U.S. Army engineers, who mingled sky-blue or gray 'shell' jackets with dark blue trousers, and oilcloth-covered forage caps as their fatigue dress when posted in the Washington, DC area during April 1861. While this and other uniforms that the troops were arrayed in during the opening months of the war provided a rich tapestry to casual observers, it violated one of the basic functions of a military uniform – identification of friend from foe. Ignoring this tenet caused such confusion that orders eventually forbade the use of any color but the established combination of light and dark blue. Even then regional differences, individual tastes and other factors continued to make variations more the rule than the exception.

Besides these coats of many colors, clothing was often condemned as 'shoddy'. This term originally meant 'a woolen yarn obtained by tearing to shreds refuse woolen rags', which was combined with some new wool to make 'a kind of cloth'. The word soon took on a different meaning as 'Worthless material made to look like material of superior quality'.

Poor quality and the tendency toward diversity in dress eventually subsided, and a certain degree of uniformity came into being, at least for the Yankees. In time, many volunteer units abandoned fanciful or impractical garb for the regular army kit or components of the outfit as set down in regulations adopted in 1861 (see the Appendix). Thus, for the most part the Northerners came to be more consistent in their basic appearance than the Southerners. Given that the former force operated under central federal control with Lincoln as commander in chief, and the latter body was made up of troops who theoretically were subject to the authority of their respective states rather than directly responsive to Jefferson Davis' Richmond government, the continued widespread variances of Confederate uniforms seemed appropriate.

This was not merely symbolic; the industrial North had a greater capability to mass produce uniforms, shoes, accouterments, and other materials required to wage war, while the chiefly agrarian South could not churn out vast quantities of war supplies. Nonetheless, the Confederates gave as good as they got. During the early years of the conflict especially, they outfought, outmaneuvered or outgeneraled the Yankees. They fought so fiercely as to make it appear that they might succeed in their bid to break from the Union.

The cost of the conflict in blood and national treasure was exceedingly high, and eventually took its toll, particularly on the front line troops. These men served as Lincoln's 'terrible swift sword'[1] to bring back the rebellious South to the fold. After four years of hard fighting and many deaths (although more men died from disease than combat) they succeeded in trampling out the grapes of wrath. Their victory reunited a nation that tragically had been torn asunder.

FOR FURTHER READING

Dyer, Frederick H., *A Compendium of the War of the Rebellion*, 2 Vols. Dayton, OH: Morningside Bookshop, 1978.

McAfee, Michael J. and Langellier, John P., *Billy Yank: The Uniform of the Union Army, 1861–1865*. London: Greenhill Books, 1996.

Todd, Frederick P., *American Military Equipage 1851–1872*, Volume II: State Forces. New York: Chatam Square Press, 1981.

Williams, T. Harry, *The History of American Wars: From Colonial Times to World War I*. New York: Alfred A. Knopf, 1981.

1. The qoutation originates from the opening stanza of *The Battle Hymn of the Republic*, an important Union song written by Harriet Beacher Stowe and published in February 1862

Right: The 1851-pattern enlisted foot overcoat was worn by infantry and artillery troops alike, in this case by a member of the latter organization, as indicated by the small brass cannon insignia on his privately purchased non-regulation hat. *RB*

Below: Light artillery officers were distinguished by their distinctive cap with falling horsetail plume and scarlet and gold cap cords. These officers carried the M1850 foot officer's sword, as seen here, or the M1840 light artillery saber. Note that the trousers are dark blue, even though light artillerymen were to have sky-blue trousers even before General Orders No. 108, Headquarters of the Army, 16 December 1861, called for the lighter hue for all troops. *MJM*

Right: Two gunners, the one on the left and the man in the center, have on the four-button sack coat so commonly seen during the Civil War, while the man on the left has modified his blouse with the addition of black velvet cuffs and collar. Such additions were not uncommon. All three have the M1840 light artillery saber. The standing soldier, a first sergeant as indicated by his chevrons with a diamond above three stripes and a scarlet worsted sash, has his saber hooked from the M1851 saber belt with rectangular belt plate displaying a spread eagle and a separately applied German silver wreath. The middle artilleryman wears the old M1840 light artillery saber belt with interlocking circular 'US' plate. This man also has an oilcloth or rubberized cap cover on his forage cap. Note the use of dark blue trousers. *NA*

Above: A typical light artillery battery stand at attention in the sky-blue kersey trousers that had been issued to their branch prior to the Civil War, and which were prescribed for all branches in accordance with General Orders No. 108, Headquarters of the Army, 16 December 1861. During the course of the war, this two-tone look tended to be in the majority, but was not always the norm. Once again, the man second from the left in the foreground has obtained a civilian slouch hat in lieu of the forage cap. *NA*

Left: Officers from the Keystone Battery of Pennsylvania (also known as Hastings' or the Tenth Parrott Battery) appear both in the short stable jacket authorized for mounted officers, including light artillery officers, and the nine-button single-breasted company-grade frock coat. Their dark blue trousers show the diversity between the hues of blue worn during the conflict. They stand in front of a 3-inch Parrott rifle. *NA*

Left: Enlisted men of the Keystone Battery gather in four-button flannel sacks and forage caps, except for a few men in the rear who have taken their blouses off and wear only their shirts. Two corporals are seated on the ground to the left of the cannon, as indicated by their scarlet chevrons with two stripes. Another corporal leans (standing) on the cannon wheel, while seated at his left hand is a sergeant with three stripes on his sleeve. Toward the rear rank on the right, a sergeant major appears, with three arcs above his stripes. Dark blue trousers are the rule here, rather than the light blue. *NA*

Left: Here members of the Keystone Battery drill with their guns. Note the limbers and caissons that made it possible for these light artillerymen to be mobile. *NA*

Left: The regulation dress uniform of a pioneer of heavy artillery, so designated by the scarlet crossed hatchets made of facing material that were worn above the elbows of the coat. The diagonal stripe is a service in war chevron which was scarlet for all troops who had served faithfully during wartime, but had sky-blue borders on each side for artillery. *USAQM*

Below: The heavy artillery musician regulation U.S. Army dress uniform included the 1858-pattern enlisted frock coat with scarlet worsted lace on the chest and sky-blue 1861-pattern trousers. The drum is suspended from a strap, which has a holder for the drumsticks. *USAQM*

Above left: The frock coats of heavy artillerymen, who were not musicians, did not have the extra lace ornamentation on the chest, as evidenced by this corporal, whose rank is designated by two scarlet lace chevrons worn points down above the elbow on either sleeve and a ½-inch stripe of worsted lace let into the outer seams of the trousers. The cap pouch for musket percussion caps is slid onto a black harness leather or black buff leather M1856 infantry belt with cast brass oval 'US' plate. *USAQM*

Above: Sergeants of heavy artillery wore three chevrons points down and 1½-inch leg stripes. They also had a special waist belt for their M1833 foot artillery sword, an edged weapon inspired by a French style that itself drew upon the ancient Roman *gladius. USAQM*

Left: Light artillery (horse or field artillery) enlisted men were to be issued the M1840 light artillery saber. Because they were mounted, these gunners also had the 1854-pattern mounted jacket with scarlet worsted lace trim and a showy cap with horsehair plume and sidelines, as is depicted here for a sergeant major. Sergeants major were distinguished by chevrons consisting of three stripes surmounted by three arcs. These were to be made of silk lace. *USAQM*

Above: Regimental quartermaster sergeant of cavalry, as indicated by his yellow silk chevrons with three stripes worn points down surmounted by three tie bars. The hat was to be looped up on the left for mounted troops, but the regulation was ignored at times. The edged weapon was to be the M1859 light cavalry saber and was worn on the M1855 saber belt that could be of buff leather dyed black or of harness leather. *USAQM*

Left: Light artillery trumpeters likewise wore the ornamental worsted lace on the chest of the jacket, as did the cavalry in yellow, dragoons in orange, and the mounted rifles in emerald green - the respective trim of these branches. *USAQM*

Above: The leather saber knot and one of several types of carbine cartridge boxes issued, depending on the model of the weapon provided, are evident in this view, as is some of the yellow worsted trim that adorned the rear of the mounted enlisted jacket of the 1854 and 1855 patterns. *USAQM*

Left: First sergeants were distinguished by three stripes worn points down with a lozenge above, as seen here for a cavalry first sergeant. The carbine sling was to be worn on the left shoulder and terminate at the right hip, the model here being in error. The carbine is a Spencer, one of many weapons carried by mounted Union troops. *USAQM*

Above: All senior NCOs, such as sergeants major of infantry who wore silk sky-blue chevrons of three stripes below three arcs, were to have a scarlet worsted sash that wrapped around the waist and tied behind the left hip. All NCOs from first sergeant upwards were permitted the sash. They were also authorized to have the M1840 NCO sword as a badge of their position, this weapon being suspended from a shoulder belt that also had provision for a bayonet scabbard. *USAQM*

Above right: The infantry musician regulation U.S. Army dress uniform included the 1858-pattern enlisted frock coat and sky-blue 1861-pattern trousers. The edged weapon was the M1840 musician's sword. *USAQM*

Right: Rear of the 1858-pattern foot soldier's frock coat, in this case for an infantry corporal whose rank was indicated by two light blue worsted stripes worn points down above the elbow. A dark blue ½-inch worsted stripe was sewn along the outer seams of the trousers for corporals as well. Note that the M1855 .58 caliber cartridge box with its oval brass 'US' plate was positioned behind the right hip and secured by the black leather waist belt. *USAQM*

Far left: In 1857 a four-button sack coat of dark blue flannel was introduced for mounted troops, and a year later the garment was made regulation for all regular army enlisted personnel as a fatigue and field item. The floppy forage cap likewise was adopted in 1858. Regulations required the company letter in stamped sheet brass for this cap, although caps were worn without any insignia or a combination of several types of insignia, including corps badges, in numerous instances. The sky-blue 1861-pattern trousers seen here became the norm relatively soon after the war began. *USAQM*

Left: A rubberized poncho was issued to keep the foot soldier dry during rain. The cavalry was supposed to have a talma (waterproof raincoat) for the same purpose, but the poncho was prevalent. *USAQM*

Far left: For cold weather a double-breasted sky-blue kersey overcoat with long cape and roll collar was to be worn by mounted troops. The foot soldier had a similar garment but with a stand-up collar, shorter cape, and of a single-breasted style. *USAQM*

Left: A long white canvas stable frock was called for to protect the uniforms of mounted troops while they performed stable duty. *USAQM*

Right: Militia and volunteers, such as these officers, wore many variations of the regular army uniform. In this case, the collars and cuffs are faced in the light blue infantry branch color prescribed by the U.S. Army Regulations of 1851. These officers may be from the Fifth California Volunteer Militia Infantry Regiment, a unit that wore such trim.

Above: At the outbreak of the Civil War the regular U.S. Army had two regiments of cavalry, whose trim was yellow, two of dragoons, whose trim was orange, and one of mounted rifles, with emerald green trim. In the last instance the riflemen were to have a green worsted hat cord on their 1858-pattern hat and a stamped sheet brass perpendicular bugle as their insignia. *Photograph by Gordon Chappell*

Left: A first sergeant of heavy artillery, with chevrons made from pieces of scarlet worsted lace individually sewn either to a cloth backing to match the coat or directly onto the sleeve, both means of application being used for NCO's stripes of the era. *RB*

Above: Officers and men from Benson's Battery man their guns behind earth works at Fair Oaks, Virginia, around 1864. A russet leather haversack to carry rounds is evident on the artilleryman fifth from the right, who also has on a 'bummer's cap' and has tucked his trousers into either his socks or his leggings. *NA*

Below: The garrison of Fort Totten, near Rock Creek Church, District of Columbia, wear short jackets, despite being a heavy artillery unit. One of the officers, who stands in front of the formation outside the reinforced earthworks structure (a magazine perhaps), has his crimson sash on over the right shoulder and tied at the left hip, indicating that he probably was serving as 'Officer of the Day'. *NA*

Above: Two trumpeters stand ready to give a bugle call at Fort Totten. Note that many of the artillerymen are wearing their brass shoulder scales, which might be retained in garrison situations such as this, but in the field were abandoned for the most part. *NA*

Below: Light artillerymen pose in front of the fortifications opposing Atlanta, Georgia in 1864. Many have stripped down to their shirts and braces (suspenders), perhaps because of the heat and humidity. One man on the ground to the right, resting against a cannon wheel hub, has on a dark civilian slouch hat with crossed artillery cannon insignia and a hat cord, instead of the forage cap worn by most of his comrades. *NA*

Right: Private C.F.W. Richert of the Twenty-third New York Independent Battery wore the complete regulation light artillery enlisted uniform, including the 1864-pattern hat, when he was photographed in that year. *MJM*

Opposite page, top: Heavy Parrott rifles on iron siege carriages could pound the rebels with merciless shelling. Note that the sergeant on the far right has the correct scarlet 1½-inch worsted lace leg stripe as well as stamped brass artillery insignia on the crown of his forage cap. Several of the other men also have brass insignia on their caps, even though only the company letter was called for by regulations. *NA*

Opposite page, bottom: A 200-pounder at Missionary Ridge with artillerymen in a mixture of short 'shell' jackets and four-button sacks with various forage caps, civilian slouch hats, and apparently some 1858-pattern issue hats. The soldier to the left front has his musket at the 'carry arms' position. *NA*

Above: A sentry keeps watch in a four-button sack coat with an M1855 cartridge box and an 1858-pattern hat, while his comrades, presumably part of the gun crew, rest outside a 'dog' tent. *NA*

Below: The officer at the left wears 'Russian knots', which were optional in lieu of the more traditional shoulder straps for light artillery officers. *NA*

Left: This light artillery private clutches an M1859 light cavalry saber. Note the brass crossed cannon artillery insignia atop his forage cap. *LC*

Below left: Although not formally permitted to enlist by the War Department prior to 1863, Blacks were recruited by some states to fight for the Union cause. Ultimately fourteen heavy artillery regiments and ten batteries of light artillery joined, the latter units often being attired in short jackets for mounted artillerymen, as seen in this image of a dapper African-American private. The jacket is not completely regulation in cut, one variation being a lower collar. *GNMP*

Below: Holding his M1859 light cavalry saber, this field-grade officer wears the standard uniform of Union majors through colonels, except for his headgear which is a non-regulation item resembling the 1858-pattern U.S. Army hat. Headgear variations were among the most common diversions from the prescribed regular army uniform during the Civil War. The gauntlets represent a practical accessory for mounted troops. Note that the trousers are still dark blue, indicating perhaps that this image was made early in the war, although the darker trousers continued to be seen alongside the light blue trousers throughout the conflict. *WCC*

Above: These officers of the Fifth U.S. Cavalry show the dark and light blue trouser choices that existed during the war, even among regular army units. Privately purchased 'porkpie' hats or straw boaters have been adopted by three of the men, while the fourth has elected to wear an officer's forage cap complete with the proper gold embroidered crossed sabers for cavalry. *NA*

Below: The Second New York Cavalry Regiment was a 'three month' regiment (a unit raised for ninety days, under the false assumption that the war would end quickly; this regiment was later redesignated the Seventh New York) that responded to the call to arms in 1861, at Troy, New York. The regimental officers in front of their men seem to be wearing regulation frock coats (single breasted for company-grade officers and double breasted for field-grade officers – majors through colonels) and matching dark blue trousers. *NA*

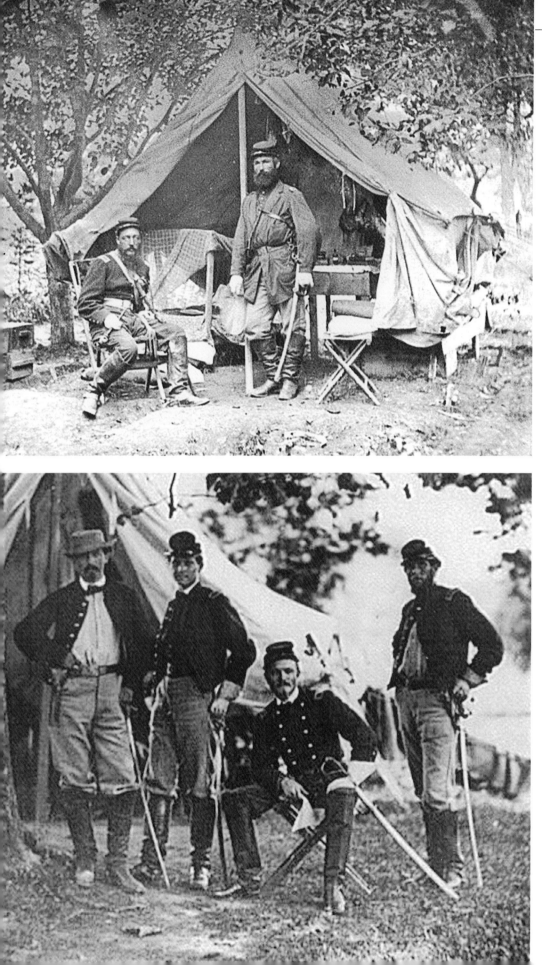

Left: During the August 1862 Peninsula Campaign Lieutenants Wright and Ford of the Third Pennsylvania Cavalry exhibit two basic garments that were popular for officers and men alike – the short jacket and the loose-fitting blouse. *LC*

Left: Another photograph taken of Third Pennsylvania Cavalry officers during the Peninsula Campaign. The regiment's colonel, William Avery, is seated in a double-breasted jacket, as called for in regulations as the proper option for field-grade officers of mounted units. Single-breasted versions were to be the norm for company-grade officers, as seen here (left to right standing) for Lieutenant W.H. Brown, Fifth U.S. Cavalry (with his light civilian slouch hat), Lieutenant H.H. King, Third Pennsylvania Cavalry, and Lieutenant Phillip Poland, Third Pennsylvania Cavalry. *LC*

Above: These Fourth Pennsylvania Cavalry officers serving in the Peninsula Campaign include Colonel James H. Childs (center), who has selected a four-button sack coat that differs from the U.S. Army pattern in its long, frock-like length. Two of the officers have bought chasseur forage caps, which were lower in the crown than the U.S. Army pattern. *LC*

Left: Corporal Nailer of the Thirteenth Pennsylvania Cavalry has kept the brass shoulder scales, and added sheet brass crossed sabers insignia and the regimental numeral to his forage cap top. His 1855-pattern jacket is open at the bottom to reveal a vest. *LC*

Above: Troops of the Thirteenth Pennsylvania Cavalry Regiment, Second Division Cavalry Corps, during March 1864, also display a mixture of 1855-pattern jackets and 1857-pattern four-button sack coats. The officer in front of the formation has a velvet collar on his jacket. *LC*

Above right: In the background the regimental standard of the Sixteenth Pennsylvania Cavalry (with the state coat of arms prominently incorporated) is unfurled as officers from this regiment offer examples of the company-grade single-breasted nine-button frock coat and field-grade double-breasted (with seven buttons in each row) frock coat along with four-button sack coats and the short jacket – all the major regulation options for Union cavalry officers. *NA*

Below: Members of the Eighteenth Pennsylvania Cavalry, Third Division Cavalry Corps, encamped during March 1864 at Brandy Station (the site of one of the most notable cavalry engagements of the Civil War), for the most part appear in shell jackets, forage caps and sky-blue trousers, although an occasional four-button sack coat or shirt is seen, as indicative of the diversity which existed even within the same unit. *LC*

Above: A trooper of the First Massachusetts Cavalry holds a mount steady, with its dark blue saddle blanket and the faint orange stripe over which is the famed M1859 McClellen saddle with its rawhide-covered seat. Note how the bottom of the four-button sack coat resembles a 'cutaway' coat in this instance. Many different versions of this versatile garment were produced during the war. *NA*

Right: Seated on the left, an unknown officer lounges in a well-tailored four-button blouse while the two officers in the center of the picture, Captains Edward Flint and Charles Francis Adams, Jr, have somewhat baggier blouses. The officer to the right is Second Lieutenant George Teague, who wears a shell jacket over his vest. Note that the forage caps bear no insignia. Adams and Teague have purchased fashionable high-top boots. All four men are of the First Massachusetts Cavalry at the siege of Petersburg. *LC*

Opposite page, top: These officers and non-commissioned officers of Companies C and D, First Massachusetts Cavalry, demonstrate the mixture of light blue and dark blue trousers that prevailed even late in the Civil War. This picture was also taken during the siege of Petersburg in August 1864. *LC*

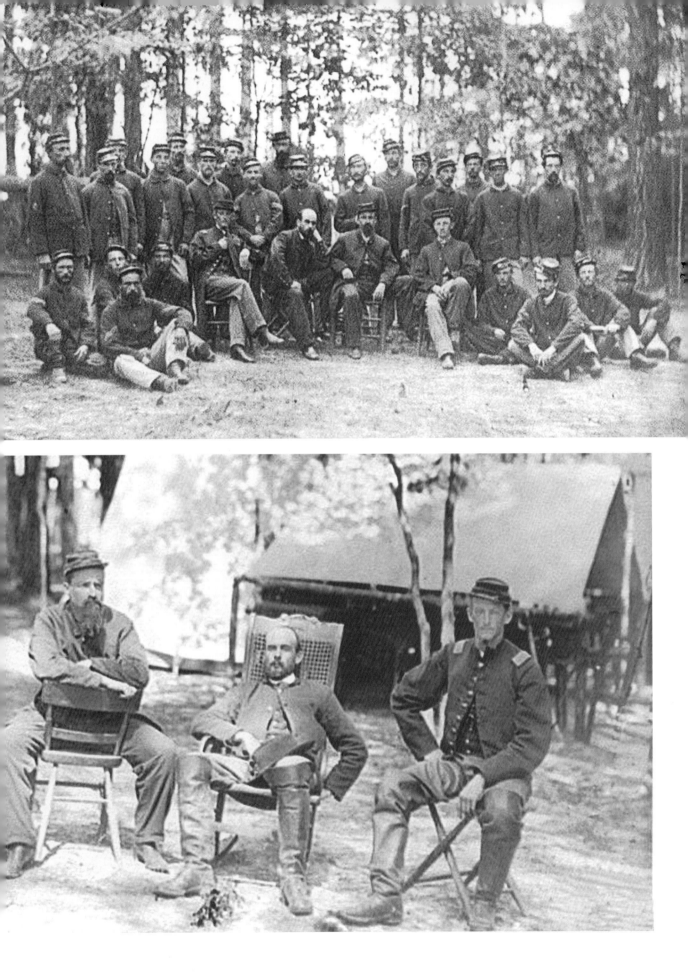

Above: These troopers from the Third Indiana Cavalry likewise are at Petersburg, Virginia, but in this case the image was made in November 1862. The collars of their jackets are lower and trimmed differently than the U.S. Army pattern. *LC*

Left: A private, possibly of the District of Columbia Cavalry, stands at ease in a twelve-button enlisted mounted jacket with yellow worsted lace adopted for cavalry enlisted men in 1855, and sky-blue kersey trousers. He has placed his cap pouch on the left side, rather than the right which was the more common placement of this accouterment. *LC*

Opposite page, top: An unknown cavalry second lieutenant, indicated by plain shoulder straps with yellow centers, strikes a Napoleonic pose in front of the Orange and Alexandria Railroad near Union Mills, Virginia. He has on a company-grade officer's mounted jacket and a civilian slouch hat. The remainder of the group seem to be a mixed assortment of cavalrymen and infantrymen. *NA*

Opposite page, bottom left: Distinct corporal's chevrons are seen on this 1855-pattern cavalry enlisted jacket. Note that the trooper has on shoulder scales, which were not common except in such instances as this where the individual was attached to a high ranking officer's headquarters, in this case that of Major General Irvin McDowell. His trousers are dark blue. *NA*

Opposite page, bottom right: This cavalry private is wearing gauntlets with short cuffs that were privately purchased. His campaign hat bears simulated embroidery brass saber insignia, more commonly worn by officers. *LC*

Opposite page, top left: Individual tastes and regional variations were not uncommon when it came to the uniform, as this unknown Yankee cavalry trooper indicates with his high, fringed Southwestern-style moccasins.

Opposite page, top right: This young lieutenant of the Fifth U.S. Infantry is representative of company-grade officers of the 1858–1861 period when dark blue trousers were to be worn. The hat is the 1858-pattern with two black ostrich feathers for company-grade officers and the intermixed black and gold hat cords. Gold epaulets were seldom seen once the war began. *MJM*

Opposite page, bottom: At the end of the war, non-commissioned officers of the Thirteenth New York Cavalry gather in their sack coats and shell jackets, the latter garments displaying a number of custom elements that vary from the standard pattern, such as the velvet collar on the soldier on the far left. Standing next to him is the regimental sergeant major, with three arcs above his yellow stripes, and fifth from left is the regimental quartermaster sergeant with three tie bars over his yellow stripes. In both instances these were to be of silk lace, although other materials may have been used. *LC*

Top right: Sergeant Thomas 'Boston' Corbett, credited after the war was over with killing John Wilkes Booth, has a brand new 'McDowell' pattern forage cap with its sloping visor, in this case evidently of patent leather. Also note the small officer's cavalry insignia on his cap crown. His shiny, high-topped cavalier style boots contrast with his rumpled four-button sack coat. The trousers display the 1½-inch yellow leg stripe of a cavalry sergeant, while the blouse reveals the yellow worsted lace sergeant's chevrons. *NA*

Right: Infantry company-grade officers in their single-breasted nine-button frocks pose along with a young musician and a servant. The officer on the right has an M1850 foot officer's sword slung from his sword belt, which is supported by an over-the-shoulder strap, as are the belts of the other two officers who appear in their frock coats. *NA*

Above: A brigadier general on horseback (center figure – indicated by a double-breasted frock with buttons grouped in twos) has both field-grade and company-grade members of his staff with him. The enlisted men have both four-button blouses and frock coats. *NA*

Below: At the outset of the war, the Sixth New York Volunteer Infantry (later retitled Wilson's Zouaves, Union Volunteer Zouaves, and other names) had gray shirts and trousers with brown civilian hats that bore a tri-color cockade. Such nondescript garb was not unusual in the opening stages of the conflict when uniform supplies were not readily available. In contrast, the officers seen here differ from the troops in adopting the dark blue single- or double-breasted frock coat, depending on rank, and forage caps. *NA*

Right: During the early part of the war militiamen from the North joined the Union cause in a wide array of uniforms, such as this private whose 1858-pattern hat cord terminates in acorns rather than the tassels of the U.S. Army design. His cuffs, collar and shoulder loops are covered in branch facings, also unlike regulars, and may indicate that he is a member of the Fifth California Militia Volunteer Infantry. The belt is the M1855 rifleman's type, just one of many versions of accouterments available to Union soldiers.

Below: Even before the Civil War erupted, French zouave outfits were all the rage with militia units both North and South. The 114th Pennsylvania (also called Collis Zouaves and originating in 1861 as independent 'Zouaves d'Afrique') was one such unit that subscribed to this fashion trend. Their jackets were dark blue with sky-blue cuffs and red lace accents. The vest was dark blue, the sash light blue, the trousers red, and medium gaiters white. Enlisted men had red fezzes with yellow tassels and white turbans, while the officers wore red forage caps with gold braid and French-style officer's uniforms consisting of a dark blue frock and red pants. They carry the M1861 Springfield rifled musket, a mainstay of Union infantrymen. This picture was taken at Petersburg in August 1864 as an example of the continued diversity of uniforms still being worn in the Union army at that late date. *LC*

Left: A wounded zouave is being tended to by an infantryman in this staged scene. The compassionate comrade wears a sky-blue kersey mounted overcoat and a protective cover on his forage cap. He also has rolled up the trousers, which are too long. Garments often did not fit when issued, and had to be tailored, causing soldiers reluctantly to use some of their meager pay. *NA*

Below: Officers of the Ninth New York Volunteer Infantry (AKA Hawkins' Zouaves, Little Zouaves or Zoo-Zoos) had scarlet French-style caps and zouave dress consisting of a blue jacket and vest trimmed in magenta or crimson, and blue trousers. The enlisted men wore the same vest and jacket with a red fez ornamented with a blue tassel, and trousers tucked into white gaiters. A turquoise sash was also prescribed. *NA*

Above: Men of the 164th New York Infantry wore zouave-type outfits similar to the Ninth New York. Tassels on the fezzes were green, as a symbol that the unit had many members of Irish, not French, ancestry. *NA*

Below: Officers of the 164th New York wore distinctive French-inspired uniforms with considerable gold lace that was showy, if not practical. Galloons on the sleeves indicated rank, as did shoulder straps. The officer second from the left has on a 'pillbox' cap that was of British origins, and had been worn unofficially for several years prior to the war and for a decade or more afterwards. *NA*

Above: In 1861, at Fort Gaines, Washington, DC, officers of the Fifty-fifth New York, an outfit made up of French residents of New York City, display their Gallic roots in uniforms that could have come directly from Paris. The overcoats were blue-gray lined and trimmed in red. Trousers were red, as were the forage caps that had blue bands and gold trim. *NA*

Below: The Twenty-second Regiment of Infantry, National Guard State of New York, adopted another French-style outfit, that of the chasseur, or French light infantry. This outfit consisted of a dark blue jacket trimmed in light blue for the men, with sky-blue pants, white epaulets with a crescent of light blue at the end, white gaiters, and a white pompon on the felt shako, or a forage cap without pompon that had quatrefoils. This photograph was taken at Harpers Ferry, Virginia. *NA*

Right: As further evidence of France's influence on early Civil War Union attire, some 10,000 chasseur de Vincennes uniforms were imported from France for issue in the United States to such Union units as the Eighty-third Pennsylvania Volunteer Infantry Regiment. This even included the leather cap or shako with cock feathers. The jackets were dark blue with yellow piping. *KSHS*

Below: Eventually the fanciful Franco-American uniforms of the Twenty-second New York were replaced by the more practical four-button sack, although chasseur-type forage caps remained in vogue, along with a number of Scottish tams that several men seemed to think just the thing for life in camp. Note the rubberized or painted canvas knapsack with regimental markings. The Yankee uniform was not constant during the war years, but changed over time. *NA*

Left: While this company-grade officer of the Fourth Michigan Infantry differs little from his counterparts in many other units, his men have succumbed to the zouave craze by adopting tassel-topped, knit caps and leather gaiters (leggings). The remainder of the uniform, however, is the common Union infantry field kit. *NA*

Below left: Some enlisted men from the Twenty-third New York found the tasseled stocking cap to their liking, although two of the privates here seem to be more comfortable with the forage cap. *NA*

Right: Various groups sought to maintain their national origins, such as some units in the Thirty-ninth New York, who called themselves the Garibaldi Guard because of the many Italians in the organization. Their *bersaglieri*-type hats bore an American eagle, however, as the headgear of the two men in the background (right) indicate. Their hats also had wide bands of red cloth to distinguish their unit further. In the foreground, a bandsman with a saxhorn has an M1840 musician's sword. His hat and that of the man to the left in the background are 1858-pattern regular army enlisted style, one with the stamped sheet brass infantry hunting horn and the other with crossed cannons of the artillery. *NA*

Below: The Irish were another prominent national group who rallied to the Union cause. One of the most famous of these units was the Sixty-ninth New York Infantry, seen here at Fort Corcoran, Virginia (named after the regimental commander, Colonel Michael Corcoran), in 1861. The uniforms are mostly the U.S. Army regulation style, although embellished by an occasional baldric or chasseur-type forage cap with gold trim. *NA*

Above: Colonel John Cochrane commanded the 65th New York Infantry Regiment. His elegant 1851-pattern officer's cloak coat or capote was lined inside, possibly in a lighter shade of blue for infantry. *NA*

Above: The Seventh New York Volunteer Infantry Regiment was one of many Union units that wore gray when the Civil War started. The trim was black, and havelocks (following the British fashion) were sometimes worn. *NA*

Left: Facings were black on the 1861-pattern Seventh New Yorkers' coats and trousers, and cross belts were white. *NA*

Left: Later in the war the Seventh New York changed over to the 1863-pattern uniform issued to troops from that state with its distinctive 'polka skirted' jacket of dark blue trimmed in white. *NA*

Above: The Twenty-third New York Volunteer Infantry carried the M1842 musket and had the dark blue 1863-pattern polka skirted jacket worn with contrasting sky-blue trousers. Note that the corporal second from the left and the sergeant inside the tent have chevrons that appear somewhat larger in the width of the tape than usual. *NA*

Left: Men of the Twenty-second New York Volunteer Infantry had Enfield muskets with saber bayonets. They began the war with gray trousers, frock coats and forage caps, and changed over to dark blue jackets piped in light blue later, as well as adopted Regular Army field garb. Note the gaiters, which are either leather or canvas. *NA*

Left: Another group of Twenty-third New Yorkers from Company D depict both the 1863-pattern blue jacket and what are probably issue, off-white flannel shirts. *NA*

Left: Private James Bonett and his comrades relax in standard issue-type shirts and other shirts, including the dark blue shirt of the style provided to troops from Massachusetts. *NA*

Right: Shirts were among the most common variations of the Yankee soldier's wardrobe, as seen in this picture of a motley group of Twenty-third New Yorkers, including one in a striped jersey! *NA*

Below: A soldier at his laundry chores has on a representative light colored shirt and bummer's cap. *NA*

Above: Shirts, four-button blouses, vests and frock coats are all combined in this camp scene, where some of the men have put aside forage caps for what appear to be forerunners of the WWI overseas cap. In many instances soft camp hats were favored for such off-duty occasions. The wide range of headgear worn by both Union and Confederate troops was a hallmark of the Civil War. Further, although these men belong to the infantry, boots have been selected rather than the shoes or brogans usually seen on foot soldiers. *NA*

Left: Braid covers the chasseur-style forage caps of this trio who perhaps are from a Union zouave unit. Note that dark shirts as well as light ones were worn both as an undergarment and in some instances as an outer garment. *NA*

Above: Officers of the Fourth New Jersey Infantry favor a variety of sack coats, although some frock coats are evident. Forage caps and civilian-type slouch hats are seen. The officer on the left wears his crimson silk sash over the shoulder, which was to indicate the officer of the day. *NA*

Below: As early as June 1862, corps badges were adopted to designate units above the regimental level, in addition to helping to build unit identity and cohesiveness. Here some officers of the 138th Pennsylvania Infantry have affixed the VI Corps badge (a cross in white for the second division) to their caps. *NA*

Above: Many of the men from Company C, 110th Pennsylvania Infantry, have affixed the diamond of the III Corps to their forage cap crowns. This unit was the first to adopt corps badges, sometimes known as the 'Kearny patch' after the individual credited with originating the concept, Major General Philip Kearny. *NA*

Left: The corporal on the right with finely made chevrons on his four-button blouse also has a pin on the chest that resembles the XX Corps, 173rd Pennsylvania Infantry provost guard badge. What is certain is that his sky-blue kersey trousers have the correct ½-inch dark blue worsted leg stripes for infantry corporals. *NA*

Right: In contrast, the chevrons of this infantry corporal are made crudely, and evidently are sewn directly onto his sack coat rather than being applied to cloth backing that is then stitched to the garment – the more common method of fabricating these non-commissioned rank devices. *NA*

Below: The infantry first sergeant on the far right has on the more traditional type of non-commissioned chevrons, with a large diamond device above to set him apart from sergeants, such as the two seated playing cards. None of these NCOs has the dark blue worsted 1½-inch stripe on their trousers, as called for in the case of all infantry sergeants. *NA*

Above: The first sergeant standing in the foreground of this group of infantrymen has on the scarlet worsted NCO sash, while his chevrons have a slightly smaller lozenge device above them. The men wear a mixture of enlisted frock coats, blouses, and even a short mounted-type jacket here and there, once again demonstrating the variations even within a company, much less for units of larger size. *NA*

Below: The seated infantry first sergeant on the left and the one in the middle have differing chevrons on their frock coat and blouse, respectively. The sergeant seated to right has no 1½-inch dark blue worsted leg stripes on his trousers. Again, boots are seen, as are the more common shoes or brogans of foot soldiers. *NA*

Above: While at first glance the seated sergeant (fifth from the right of this camp scene) has on his chevrons with points down per regulations, there are four stripes, not the regulation three, below his diamond. Additionally, the corporal at the far left wears his chevrons points up, contrary to regulations. *NA*

Below: Another first sergeant at the left of this winter camp scene likewise is obvious by his chevrons. The man at the right foreground leaning against a log structure has obtained an 1851-pattern sky-blue kersey mounted overcoat, rather than the foot soldier's greatcoat that would usually be issued to infantrymen. *NA*

Above: The 1851-pattern dismounted overcoat with standing collar is shown here by the man to the right in this mixed group of court martial candidates from the Army of the Cumberland. They are devoid of insignia, although the man seated second from the right has a XII Corps badge on his blouse. *NA*

Below: The length of officer's frock coats ranged from mid-thigh to extending nearly to the knee. The company-grade officer (fourth from the right) with enlisted men at a sutler's store wears a long version of the somber frock appropriate to his rank. *NA*

Right: The Second Rhode Island Infantry could be identified by their distinct, long, loose pullover shirt-blouses that to some degree resembled old style 'hunting shirts'. His cap bears a regimental number '2'. *NA*

Below: The length of sack coats also ran from short to long, as the officer standing front and center of his infantry company depicts. The blouse is nearly as long as the frock coat worn by the other officer to the left. *NA*

Left: Another member of the Second Rhode Island Volunteer Infantry has a brass 'D' on his forage cap to mark him as a member of Company D. The matter of headgear insignia was just one more example of how individual tastes and the variation from regulations existing from one unit to the next gave anything but a uniform appearance. *NA*

Below: Several versions of insignia on the headgear of these Veteran Volunteer infantrymen, along with the number of hat and cap types, characterized the Civil War Yankee as a fighting man who followed personal concepts of martial attire as much as regulations. *NA*

Opposite page, top: Men of Company A, Ninth Indiana Infantry eschew the bummer's cap for felt hats, most of which are in dark hues, although the sergeant at the far right, in front of the line, has obtained a light-colored version. *NA*

Opposite page, bottom: A company of the Twenty-first Michigan Infantry stand in their plain, practical four-button blouses, and likewise preferred wide-brimmed slouch hats for combat. *NA*

Above: Men of the Fourth Michigan Infantry demonstrate how the collar of the common four-button sack coat could be worn rolled down or standing up depending on individual preferences or variations of construction. The regulation forage cap is the unanimous choice here. *NA*

Left: Perhaps these are regulars or men of the 'Iron Brigade'. In either instance they wear the 1858-pattern hat combined with sky-blue kersey trousers and the 1858-pattern infantry enlisted frock coat. *NA*

Right: Sergeant (so indicated by the three light blue worsted stripes on his sleeves) George Koch of the Sixty-ninth Regiment U.S. Colored Troops wears a typical bummer's cap and four-button sack coat, on which the stitching for the interior pocket on his left side is visible. During the war there were over 140 companies of Union infantry manned by African American enlisted personnel. *GNMP*

Right: Infantrymen outside their meager quarters likewise mostly wear the 1858-pattern infantry frock coat with shoulder scales, including a musician's coat with the light blue worsted lace on the chest. Many of the men have placed stamped sheet brass insignia on the tops of their forage caps as well. *NA*

Above: An infantry first sergeant in the regulation 1858-pattern frock coat with worsted chevrons and piping on the collar and cuffs, both in light blue. *LC*

Right: This first sergeant of Company G, Seventy-seventh Regiment U.S. Colored Troops (a unit first formed in Louisiana as the Fifth Regiment Infantry, Corps d'Afrique) appears in picture-perfect regulation dress for infantry (except his hat is looped on the right, which was prescribed for mounted troops), including the 1858-pattern frock coat topped by brass shoulder scales, the latter accessory often being abandoned during the war. His M1840 NCO sword is suspended from a belt frog rather than the over-the-shoulder belt that was the more common accouterment for this purpose. His light blue worsted chevrons surmounted by a lozenge were the prescribed rank for infantry first sergeants. *GNMP*

Left: Members of the Fourth Regiment U.S. Colored Troops stand at parade rest armed with Springfield .58 caliber rifled muskets and wearing forage caps at Fort Lincoln, one of the defense works built around Washington, DC. The first sergeant on the left wears the short jacket that was usually reserved for mounted troops and officers, while most of the other men wear the 1858-pattern infantry frock coat. There are no trouser stripes on the sergeant's outer seams – one more departure from regulations. *LC*

Opposite page, top: According to the 1861 regulations, the 1858-pattern frock coats of infantry bandsmen were to be ornamented with light blue worsted lace. Regulations also allowed additions to the regimental band uniforms, such as the sergeants' leg stripes worn by these martial musicians at a formation. *NA*

Opposite page, bottom: Once again sergeants' leg stripes are evident on these infantry fifers and drummers who likewise wear the 1858-pattern musician's frock coat. *NA*

Above: The leader of this infantry fife and drum corps has adapted regimental quartermaster sergeant chevrons as his insignia, adding a star or other device in between the tie bars and stripes. He also has an M1840 NCO sword. All men in the group have scarlet worsted NCO's sashes. *NA*

Below: Not only does the leader of this fife and drum corps have an M1840 NCO sword, but he also seems to have an infantry officer's cap device on his forage cap, along with a short jacket. All the other men wear the frock coat. The M1840 musician sword is also seen hanging from the hip of a number of the men. *NA*

Left: The youthful drum major of the Ninety-third New York Infantry's fife and drum corps has likewise opted for a short jacket, as has at least one other musician in the group. The rest of the men have a mixture of four-button blouses and 1858-pattern nine-button frocks with the musician's lace on the chest. *LC*

Above: In many instances infantry drums were painted with the Union eagle on a light blue background, as seen here with this trio of drummers from the Second Rhode Island Infantry. *NA*

Left: A proud drummer rests on the M1840 musician sword. His instrument bears a hand-painted motif with a prominent Union shield.

Above: Officers' buttons for infantry, artillery and cavalry. The larger size was for the coat and the smaller size for cuffs, vests and sometimes for jackets.

Below: Ornaments embroidered in regulation gold with silver embroidered numerals for officers' cap and hat insignia.

Below right: Officers' black silk braid for the 1851-pattern overcoat to indicate rank.

Opposite page, top: Officers' shoulder straps were to have a scarlet background for artillery, yellow for cavalry, orange for dragoons, blue for infantry, and emerald green for mounted rifles. The outer edges were gold and the bars for captains and first lieutenants were gold as well.

Opposite page, bottom left: Officers' rank insignia for epaulets.

Opposite page, bottom right: These examples of corps badges indicate that the various divisions of a corps were set off by color while the design was used to represent the corps. Badges were made of cloth, although metal versions were also produced.

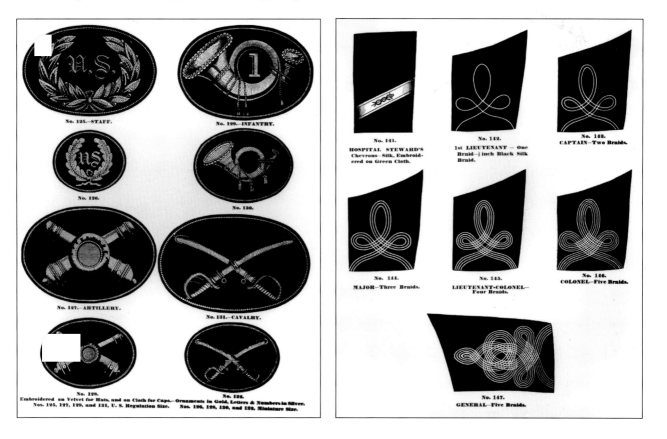

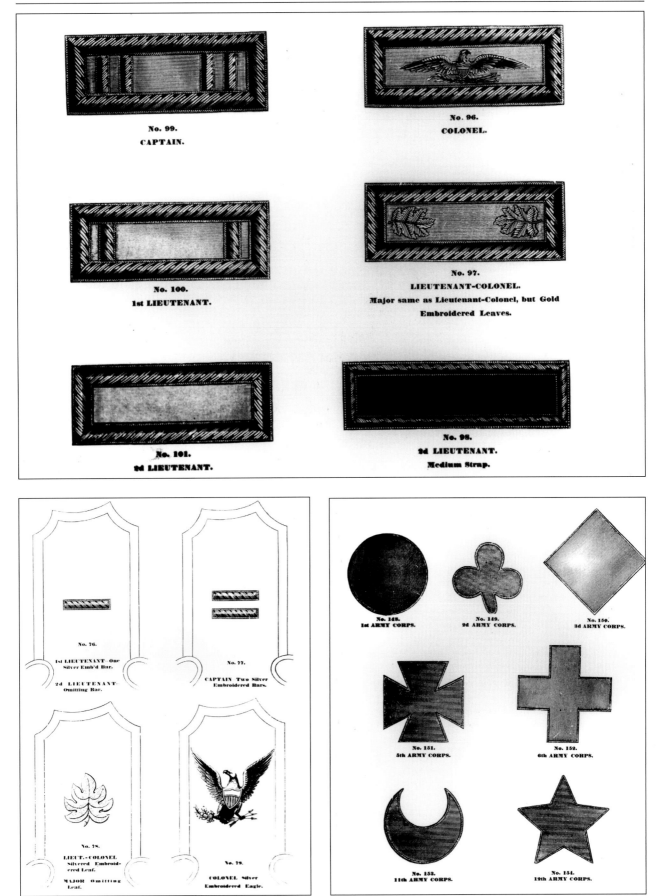

No. 99.
CAPTAIN.

No. 96.
COLONEL.

No. 100.
1st LIEUTENANT.

No. 97.
LIEUTENANT-COLONEL.
Major same as Lieutenant-Colonel, but Gold
Embroidered Leaves.

No. 101.
2d LIEUTENANT.

No. 98.
2d LIEUTENANT.
Medium Strap.

No. 76.
1st LIEUTENANT—One
Silver Emb'd Bar.
2d LIEUTENANT—
Omitting Bar.

No. 77.
CAPTAIN Two Silver
Embroidered Bars.

No. 78.
LIEUT.-COLONEL
Silvered Embroid-
ered Leaf.
MAJOR Omitting
Leaf.

No. 79.
COLONEL Silver
Embroidered Eagle.

No. 148.
1st ARMY CORPS.

No. 149.
2d ARMY CORPS.

No. 150.
3d ARMY CORPS.

No. 151.
5th ARMY CORPS.

No. 152.
6th ARMY CORPS.

No. 153.
11th ARMY CORPS.

No. 154.
12th ARMY CORPS.

APPENDIX
UNIFORM AND DRESS OF THE ARMY OF THE UNITED STATES, 1861

GENERAL ORDERS No. 6, WAR DEPARTMENT, ADJUTANT GENERAL'S OFFICE

Washington, March 13, 1861.

The UNIFORM, DRESS AND HORSE EQUIPMENTS OF THE ARMY having been changed in many respects since the 'General Regulations' of 1857, the following description of them is published for the information of all concerned:

COAT.

For Commissioned Officers.

1. All officers shall wear a frock coat of dark blue cloth, the skirt to extend from two-thirds to three-fourths of the distance from the top of the hip to the bend of the knee; single-breasted for Captains and Lieutenants; double-breasted for all other grades.

2. *For a Major General* – two rows of buttons on the breast, nine in each row, placed by threes; the distance between each row, five and one-half inches at top, and three and one-half inches at bottom; stand-up collar, to rise no higher than to permit the chin to turn freely over it, to hook in front at the bottom, and slope thence up and backward at an angle of thirty degrees on each side; cuffs two and one-half inches deep to go around the sleeves parallel with the lower edge, and to button with three small buttons at the under seam; pockets in the folds of the skirts, with one button at the hip, and one at the end of each pocket, making four buttons on the back and skirt of the coat, the hip button to range with the lowest buttons on the breast; collar and cuffs to be of dark blue velvet; lining of the coat black.

3. *For a Brigadier General* – the same as for a Major General, except that there will be only eight buttons in each row on the breast, placed in pairs.

4. *For a Colonel* – the same as for a Major General, except that there will be only seven buttons in each row on the breast, placed at equal distances; collar and cuffs of the same color and material as the coat.

5. *For a Lieutenant Colonel* – the same as for a Colonel.

6. *For a Major* – the same as for a Colonel.

7. *For a Captain* – the same as for a Colonel, except that there will be only one row of nine buttons on the breast, placed at equal distances.

8. *For a First Lieutenant* – the same as for a Captain.

9. *For a Second Lieutenant* – the same as for a Captain.

10. *For a Brevet Second Lieutenant* – the same as for a Captain.

11. A round jacket, according to pattern, of dark blue cloth, trimmed with scarlet, with the Russian shoulder-knot, the prescribed insignia of rank to be worked in silver in the center of the knot, may be worn on undress duty by officers of the light artillery.

12. The uniform coat for all enlisted *foot* men, shall be a single-breasted frock coat of dark blue cloth, made without plaits, with skirt extending one-half the distance from the top of the hip to the bend of the knee; one row of nine buttons on the breast placed at equal distances; stand-up collar to rise no higher than to permit the chin to turn freely over it, to hook in front at the bottom and then to slope up and backward at an angle of thirty degrees on each side; cuffs pointed according to pattern, and to button with two small buttons at the under seam; collar and cuffs edged with a cord or welt of cloth as follows, to wit: scarlet *for Artillery*; sky-blue *for Infantry*; yellow *for Engineers*; crimson *for Ordnance* and *Hospital stewards*. On each shoulder a metallic scale according to pattern; narrow lining for skirt of the coat of the same color and material as the coat; pockets in the folds of the skirt with one button at each hip to range with the lowest buttons on the breast; no buttons at the end of pockets.

13. *All Enlisted Men of Dragoons, Cavalry, Mounted Rifles, and Light Artillery*, shall wear a uniform jacket of dark blue cloth, with one row of twelve small buttons on the breast placed equal distances; stand-up collar to rise no higher than to permit the chin to turn freely over it, to hook in front at the bottom, and to slope the same as the coat collar; on the collar, on each side, two blind buttons holes of lace, three-eighths of an inch wide, and a strip of the same extending down the front and around the whole lower edge of the jacket; the back seam laced with same, and on the cuff a point of the same shape as that on the coat, but formed of the lace; jacket to extend to the waist, and to be lined with white flannel; two small buttons at the under seam of the cuff, as on the coat cuff; one hook and eye at the bottom of the collar; color of lace, (worsted,) orange for *Dragoons*, yellow for *Cavalry*, green for *Riflemen*, and scarlet for *Light Artillery*.

14. *For all Musicians* – the same as for other enlisted men of their respective corps, with the addition of a facing of lace three-eighths of an inch wide on the front of the coat or jackets made in the following manner: bars of three-eighths of an inch worsted lace placed on a line with each button six and one-half inches wide at the bottom, and thence gradually expanding upwards to the last button, counting from the waist up, and contracting from thence to the bottom of the collar, where it will be six and one-half inches wide, with a strip of the same lace following the bars at their outer extremity – the whole presenting something of what is called the herring-bone form; the color of the lace facing to correspond with the color of the trimming of the corps.

15. *For Fatigue Purposes* – a sack coat of dark blue flannel extending half way down the thigh, and made loose, without sleeve or body lining, falling collar, inside pocket on the left side, four coat buttons down the front.

16. *For Recruits* – the sack coat will be made with sleeve and body lining, the latter of flannel.

17. On all occasions of duty, except fatigue, and when out of quarters, the coat or jacket shall be buttoned and hooked at the collar.

BUTTONS.

18. *For General Officers and Officers of the General Staff* – gilt, convex, with spread eagle and stars, and plain border; large size, seven-eighths of an inch in exterior diameter; small size one-half inch.

19. *For Officers of the Corps of Engineers* – gilt, nine-tenths of an inch in exterior diameter, slightly convex; a raised bright rim, one-thirtieth of an inch wide; device, an eagle holding in his beak a scroll, with the word 'Essayons', a bastion with embrasures in the distance surrounded by water, with a rising sun – the figures to be of dead gold upon a bright field. Small buttons of the same form and device, and fifty-five hundredths of an inch in exterior diameter.

20. *For Officers of the Corps of Topographical Engineers* – gilt, seven-eighths of an inch exterior diameter, convex and solid; device, the shield of the United States, occupying one-half the diameter, and the letters T.E. in old English characters the other half; small buttons, one-half inch diameter, device and form the same.

21. *For Officers of the Ordnance Department* – gilt, convex, plain border, cross cannon and bombshell, with a circular scroll over and across the cannon, containing the words 'Ordnance Corps'; large size, seven-eighths of an inch in exterior diameter; small size, one-half inch.

22. *For Officers of Artillery, Infantry, Riflemen, Cavalry, and Dragoons* – gilt, convex; device, a spread eagle with the letter A, for Artillery – I, for Infantry – R, for Riflemen – C, for Cavalry – D, for Dragoons, on the shield; large size, seven-eighths of an inch in exterior diameter; small size, one-half inch.

23. *Aides-de-camp* may wear the button of the General Staff, or of their regiment or corps, at their option.

24. *For all Enlisted Men* – yellow, the same as is used by the Artillery, &c., omitting the letter in the shield.

TROUSERS.

25. *For General Officers and Officers of the Ordnance Department* – of dark blue cloth, plain, without stripe, welt, or cord down the outer seam.

26. *For Officers of the General Staff and Staff Corps*, except the Ordnance – dark blue cloth, with a gold cord, one-eighth of an inch diameter, along the outer seam.

27. *For all Regimental Officers* – dark blue cloth, with a welt let into the outer seam, one-eighth of an inch in diameter, of colors corresponding to the facings of the respective regiments, viz: *Dragoons*, orange; *Cavalry*, yellow; *Riflemen*, emerald green; *Artillery*, scarlet; *Infantry*, sky-blue.

28. *For Enlisted Men*, except companies of Light Artillery – dark blue cloth; sergeants with a stripe one and one-half inch wide; corporals with a stripe one-half inch wide, of worsted lace, down and over the outer seam, of the color of the facings of the respective corps.

29. *Ordnance Sergeants and Hospital Stewards* – stripe of crimson lace one and one-half inch wide.

30. *Privates* – plain, without stripe or welt.

31. *For Companies of Artillery equipped as Light Artillery* – sky-blue cloth.

All trousers to be made loose, without plaits, and to spread well over the boot; to be re-enforced for all enlisted mounted men.

HAT.

32. *For Officers* – of best black felt. The dimensions of medium size to be as follows:
Width of brim, 3¼ inches,
Height of crown, 6¼ inches,
Oval of tip, ½ inch,
Taper of crown, ¾ inch,
Curve of head, ⅜ inch.
The binding to be ½-inch deep, of best black ribbed silk.

33. *For Enlisted Men* – of black felt, same shape and size as for officers, with double row of stitching, instead of binding, around the edge. To agree in quality with the pattern deposited in the clothing arsenal.

Trimmings.

34. *For General Officers* – gold cord, with acorn-shaped ends. The brim of the hat looped up on the right side, and fastened with an eagle attached to the side of the hat; three black ostrich feathers on the left side; a gold embroidered wreath in front, on black velvet ground, encircling the letters U.S. in silver, old English characters.

35. *For Officers of the Adjutant General's, Inspector General's, Quartermaster's, Subsistence, Medical and Pay Departments, and the Judge Advocate, above the rank of Captain* – the same as for General Officers, except the cord which will be of black silk and gold.

36. *For the same Departments, below the rank of Field Officers* – the same as for Field Officers, except that there will be but two feathers.

37. *For Officers of the Corps of Engineers* – the same as for the General Staff, except the ornament in front, which will be a gold embroidered wreath of laurel and palm, encircling a silver turreted castle on black velvet ground.

38. *For Officers of the Topographical Engineers* – the same as for the General Staff, except the ornament in front, which will be a gold embroidered wreath of oak leaves, encircling a gold embroidered shield, on black velvet ground.

39. *For Officers of the Ordnance Department* – the same as for the General Staff, except the ornament in front, which will be a gold embroidered shell and flame, on black velvet ground.

40. *For Officers of Dragoons* – the same as for the General Staff, except the ornament in front, which will be two gold embroidered sabers crossed, edges upward, on black velvet ground, with the number of the regiment in silver in the upper angle.

41. *For Officers of Cavalry* – the same as for the Dragoons, except that the number of the regiment will be in the lower angle.

42. *For Officers of Mounted Riflemen* – the same as for the General Staff, except the ornament in front, which will be a gold embroidered trumpet, perpendicular, on black velvet ground.

43. *For Officers of Artillery* – the same as for the General Staff, except the ornament in front, which will be gold embroidered cross-cannon, on black velvet ground, with the number of the regiment in silver at the intersection of the cross-cannon.

44. *For Officers of Infantry* – the same as for Artillery, except the ornament in front, which will be a gold embroidered bugle, on black velvet ground, with the number of the regiment in silver within the bend.

45. *For Enlisted Men*, except companies of Light Artillery – the same as for Officers of the respective corps, except that there will be but one feather, the cord will be of worsted, of the same color as that of the facing of the corps, three-sixteenths of an inch in diameter, running three times through a slide of the same material, and terminating with two tassels, not less than two inches long, on the side of the hat opposite the feather. For Hospital Stewards the cord will be of buff and green mixed. The insignia of corps, in brass, in front of the hat, corresponding with those prescribed for Officers, with the number of regiment, five-eighths of an inch long, in brass, and letter of company, one inch, in brass, arranged over insignia. Brim to be looped up to side of hat with a brass eagle, having a hook attached to the bottom to secure the brim – on the right side for mounted men and left side for foot men. The feather to be worn on the side opposite the loop.

46. All the trimmings of the hat are to be made so that they can be detached; but the eagle, badge of corps, and letter of company, are to be always worn.

47. For companies of Artillery equipped as Light Artillery, the old pattern uniform cap, with red horse-hair plume, cord and tassel.

48. Officers of the General Staff, and Staff Corps, may wear, at their option, a light French chapeau, either stiff crown or flat, according to the pattern deposited in the Adjutant General's Office. Officers below the rank of Field Officers to wear but two feathers.

FORAGE CAPS.

49. For fatigue purposes, forage caps, of pattern in the Quartermaster General's Office – dark blue cloth, with a welt of the same around the crown, and yellow metal letters in front to designate companies.

50. Commissioned Officers may wear forage caps of the same pattern, with the distinctive ornament of the corps and regiment in front.

CRAVAT OR STOCK.

51. *For all Officers* – black; when a cravat is worn, the tie not to be visible at the opening of the collar.

52. *For all Enlisted Men* – black leather, according to pattern.

BOOTS.

53. *For all Officers* – ankle or Jefferson.

54. *For Enlisted Men of Riflemen, Dragoons, Cavalry, and Light Artillery* – ankle and Jefferson, rights and lefts, according to pattern.

55. *For Enlisted Men of Artillery, Infantry, Engineers, and Ordnance* – Jefferson, rights and lefts, according to pattern.

SPURS.

56. *For all Mounted Officers* – yellow metal, or gilt.

57. *For all Enlisted Mounted Men* – yellow metal, according to pattern. (See No. 174.)

GLOVES.

58. *For General Officers and Officers of the General Staff and Staff Corps* – buff or white.

59. *For Officers of Artillery, Infantry, Cavalry, Dragoons, and Riflemen* – white.

SASH.

60. *For General Officers* – buff, silk net, with silk bullion fringe ends; sash to go twice around the waist, and to tie behind the left hip, pendent part not to extend more than eighteen inches below the tie.

61. *For Officers of the Adjutant General's, Inspector General's, Quartermaster's, and Subsistence Departments, Corps of Engineers, Topographical Engineers, Ordnance, Artillery, Infantry, Cavalry, Riflemen, and Dragoons, and the Judge Advocate of the Army* – crimson silk net; *for Officers of the Medical Department* – medium or emerald green silk net, with silk bullion fringe ends; to go around the waist and tie as for General Officers.

62. *For all Sergeant Majors, Quartermaster Sergeants, Ordnance Sergeants, First Sergeants, Principal or Chief Musicians and Chief Buglers* – red worsted sash, with worsted bullion fringe ends; to go twice around the waist, and to tie behind the left hip, pendent part not to extend more than eighteen inches below the tie.

63. The sash will be worn (over the coat) on all occasions of duty of every description, except stable and fatigue.

64. The sash will be worn by 'Officers of the Day' across the body, scarf fashion, from the right shoulder to the left side, instead of around the waist, tying behind the left hip as prescribed.

SWORD BELT.

65. *For all Officers* – a waist belt not less than one and one-half inch, nor more than two inches wide; to be worn over the sash; the sword to be suspended from it by slings of the same material as the belt, with a hook attached to the belt upon which the sword may be hung.

66. *For General Officers* – Russian leather, with three stripes of gold embroidery; the slings embroidered on both sides.

67. *For all other Officers* – black leather, plain.

68. *For all Non-commissioned Officers* – black leather, plain.

SWORD-BELT PLATE.

69. *For all Officers and Enlisted Men* – gilt, rectangular, two inches wide, with a raised bright rim; a silver wreath of laurel encircling the 'Arms of the United States'; eagle, shield, scroll, edge of cloud and rays bright. The motto, 'E PLURIBUS UNUM', in silver letters, upon the scroll; stars also of silver; according to pattern.

SWORD AND SCABBARD.

70. *For General Officers* – straight sword, gilt hilt, silver grip, brass or steel scabbard.

71. *For Officers of the Adjutant General's, Inspector General's, Quartermaster's, and Subsistence Departments, Corps of Engineers, Topographical Engineers, Ordnance, the Judge Advocate of the Army, Aides-de-Camp, Field Officers of Artillery, Infantry, and Foot Riflemen, and for the Light Artillery* – the sword of the pattern adopted by the War Department, April 9, 1850; or the one described in G.O. No. 21, of August 28, 1860, for officers therein designated.

72. *For the Medical and Pay Departments* – small sword and scabbard, according to pattern in the Surgeon General's office.

73. *For Officers of Dragoons, Cavalry, and Mounted Riflemen* – saber and scabbard now in use, according to pattern in the Ordnance Department.

74. *For the Artillery, Infantry, and Foot Riflemen*, except the field officers – the sword of the pattern adopted by the War Department, April 9, 1850.

75. The sword and sword belt will be worn upon all occasions of duty, without exception.

76. When on foot, the saber will be suspended from the hook attached to the belt.

77. When not on military duty, officers may wear swords of honor, or the prescribed sword, with a scabbard, gilt, or of leather with gilt mountings.

SWORDKNOT.

78. *For General Officers* – gold cord with acorn end.

79. *For all other Officers* – gold lace strap with gold bullion tassel.

BADGES TO DISTINGUISH RANK.
Epaulettes.

80. *For the Major General Commanding the Army* – gold, with solid crescent; device, three silver-embroidered stars, one, one and a half inches in diameter, one, one and one-fourth inches in diameter, and one, one and one-eighth inches in diameter, placed on the strap in a row, longitudinally, and equidistant, the largest star in the center of the crescent, the smallest at the top; dead and bright gold bullion, one-half inch in diameter and three and one-half inches long.

81. *For all other Major Generals* – the same as for the Major General Commanding the Army, except that there will be two stars on the strap instead of three, omitting the smallest.

82. *For a Brigadier General* – the same as for a Major General, except that, instead of two, there shall be one, star (omitting the smallest,) placed upon the strap, and not within the crescent.

83. *For a Colonel* – the same as for a Brigadier General, substituting a silver-embroidered spread eagle for the star upon the strap; and within the crescent for the *Medical Department* – a laurel wreath embroidered in gold, and the letters M.S., in old English characters, in silver, within the wreath; *Pay Department* – same as the Medical Department, with the letters P.D. in old English characters; *Corps of Engineers* – a turreted castle of silver; *Corps of Topographical Engineers* – a shield embroidered in gold, and below it the letters T.E., in old English characters, in silver; *Ordnance Department* – shell and flame in silver embroidery; *Regimental Officers* – the number of the regiment embroidered in gold, within a circlet of embroidered silver, one and three-fourths inches in diameter, upon cloth of the following colors: for *Artillery* – scarlet; *Infantry* – light or sky-blue; *Riflemen* – medium or emerald green; *Dragoons* – orange; *Cavalry* – yellow.

84. *For a Lieutenant Colonel* – the same as for a Colonel, according to corps, but substituting for the eagle a silver-embroidered leaf.

85. *For a Major* – the same as for a Colonel, according to corps, omitting the eagle.

86. *For a Captain* – the same as for a Colonel, according to corps, except that the bullion will be only one-fourth of an inch in diameter, and two and one-half inches long, and substituting for the eagle two silver-embroidered bars.

87. *For a First Lieutenant* – the same as for a Colonel, according to corps, except that the bullion will be only one-eighth of an inch in diameter, and two and one-half inches long, and substituting for the eagle one silver embroidered bar.

88. *For a Second Lieutenant* – the same as for a First Lieutenant, omitting the bar.

89. *For a Brevet Second Lieutenant* – the same as for a Second Lieutenant.

90. All officers having military rank will wear an epaulette on each shoulder.

91. The epaulette may be dispensed with when not on duty, and on certain duties off parade, to wit: at drills, at inspections of barracks and hospitals, on Courts of Inquiry and Boards, at inspections of articles and necessaries, on working parties and fatigue duties, and upon the march, except when, in war, there is immediate expectation of meeting the enemy, and also when the overcoat is worn.

Shoulder Straps.

92. *For the Major General Commanding the Army* – dark blue cloth, one and three-eighths inches wide by four inches long; bordered with an embroidery of gold one-fourth of an inch wide; three silver-embroidered stars of five rays, one star on the center of the strap, and one on each side equidistant between the center and the outer edge of the strap; the center star to be the largest.

93. *For all other Major Generals* – the same as for the Major General Commanding the Army, except that there will be two stars instead of three; the center of each star to be one inch from the outer edge of the gold embroidery on the ends of the strap; both stars of the same size.

94. *For a Brigadier General* – the same as for a Major General, except that there will be one star instead of two; the center of the star to be equidistant from the outer edge of the embroidery on the ends of the strap.

95. *For a Colonel* – the same size as for a Major General, and bordered in like manner with an embroidery of gold; a silver-embroidered spread eagle on the center of the strap, two inches between the tips of the wings, having in the right talon an olive branch, and in the left a bundle of arrows; an escutcheon on the breast, as represented in the arms of the United States; cloth of the strap as follows: for the *General Staff and Staff Corps* – dark blue;

Artillery – scarlet; *Infantry* – light or sky-blue; *Riflemen* – medium or emerald green; *Dragoons* – orange; *Cavalry* – yellow.

96. *For a Lieutenant Colonel* – the same as for a Colonel, according to corps, omitting the eagle, and introducing a silver-embroidered leaf at each end, each leaf extending seven-eighths of an inch from the end border of the strap.

97. *For a Major* – the same as for a Colonel, according to corps, omitting the eagle, and introducing a gold-embroidered leaf at each end, each leaf extending seven-eighths of an inch from the end border of the strap.

98. *For a Captain* – the same as for a Colonel, according to corps, omitting the eagle, and introducing at each end two gold-embroidered bars of the same width as the border, placed parallel to the ends of the strap; the distance between them and from the border equal to the width of the border.

99. *For a First Lieutenant* – the same as for a Colonel, according to corps, omitting the eagle, and introducing at each end one gold-embroidered bar of the same width as the border, placed parallel to the ends of the strap, at a distance from the border equal to its width.

100. *For a Second Lieutenant* – the same as for a Colonel, according to corps, omitting the eagle.

101. *For a Brevet Second Lieutenant* – the same as for a Second Lieutenant.

102. The shoulder strap will be worn whenever the epaulette is not.

103. The rank of non-commissioned officers will be marked by chevrons upon both sleeves of the uniform coat and overcoat, above the elbow, of silk worsted binding one half an inch wide, same color as the edging on the coat, points down, as follows:

104. *For a Sergeant Major* – three bars and an arc, in silk.

105. *For a Quartermaster Sergeant* – three bars and a tie, in silk.

106. *For an Ordnance Sergeant* – three bars and a star, in silk.

107. *For a Hospital Steward* – a caduceus two inches long, embroidered with yellow silk on each arm above the elbow, in the place indicated for a chevron, the head toward the outer seam of the sleeve.

108. *For a First Sergeant* – three bars and a lozenge, in worsted.

109. *For a Sergeant* – three bars, in worsted.

110. *For a Corporal* – two bars, in worsted.

111. *For a Pioneer* – two crossed hatchets of cloth, same color and material as the edging of the collar, to be sewed on each arm above the elbow in the place indicated for a chevron, (those of a corporal to be just above and resting on the chevron,) the head of the hatchet upward, its edges outward, of he following dimensions, viz.: *Handle* – four and one half inches long, one-fourth to one-third of an inch wide. *Hatchet* – two inches long, one inch at the edge.

112. *To indicate service* – all non-commissioned officers, musicians, and privates, who have served faithfully for the term of five years, will wear, as a mark of distinction, upon both sleeves of the uniform coat, below the elbow, a diagonal half chevron, one-half an inch wide, extending from seam to seam, the front end nearest the cuff, and one-half an inch above the point of the cuff, to be of the same color as the edging of the coat. In like manner, an additional half chevron, above and parallel to the first, for every subsequent five years of faithful service: distance between each chevron one-fourth of an inch. Service in war will be indicated by a light or sky-blue stripe on each side of the chevron for Artillery, and a red stripe for all other corps, the stripe to be one-eighth of an inch wide.

OVERCOAT.
For Commissioned Officers.

113. A *'cloak coat'* of dark blue cloth, closing by means of four frog buttons of black silk and loops of black silk cord down the breast,

and at the throat by a long loop *a echelle*, without tassel or plate, on the left side, and a black silk frog button on the right; cord for the loops fifteen-hundredths of an inch in diameter; back, a single piece, slit up from the bottom, from fifteen to seventeen inches, according to the height of the wearer, and closing at will, by buttons, and button-holes cut in a concealed flap; collar of the same color and material as the coat, rounded at the edges, and to stand or fall; when standing, to be about five inches high; sleeves loose, of a single piece, and round at the bottom, without cuff or slit; lining, woolen; around the front and lower border, the edges of the pockets, the edges of the sleeves, collar, and slit in the back, a flat braid of black silk one-half an inch wide; and around each frog button on the breast, a knot two and one-quarter inches in diameter of black silk cord, seven-hundredths of an inch in diameter, arranged according to drawing; cape of the same color and material as the coat, removable at the pleasure of the wearer, and reaching to the cuff of the coat-sleeve when the arm is extended; coat to extend down the leg from six to eight inches below the knee, according to height. *To indicate rank*, there will be on both sleeves, near the lower edge, a knot of flat black silk braid not exceeding one-eighth of an inch in width, arranged according to drawing, and composed as follows:

114. *For a General* - of five braids, double knot.
115. *For a Colonel* - of five braids, single knot.
116. *For a Lieutenant Colonel* - of four braids, single knot.
117. *For a Major* - of three braids, single knot.
118. *For a Captain* - of two braids, single knot.
119. *For a First Lieutenant* - of one braid, single knot.
120. *For a Second Lieutenant and Brevet Second Lieutenant* - a plain sleeve, without knot or ornament.

For Enlisted Men.

121. *For all Mounted Corps* - of sky-blue cloth; stand and fall collar; double breasted; cape to reach down to the cuff of the coat when the arm is extended, and to button all the way up; buttons (24.)
122. *All other enlisted men* - of sky-blue cloth; stand-up collar; single-breasted; cape to reach down to the elbows when the arm is extended, and to button all the way up; buttons (24.)
123. *For Dragoons, Cavalry, and Mounted Riflemen* - a gutta percha talma, or cloak extending to the knee, with long sleeves.

OTHER ARTICLES OF CLOTHING AND EQUIPMENT.

124. *Flannel shirt, drawers, stockings, and stable frock* - the same as now furnished.
125. *Blanket* - woolen, gray, with letters U.S. in black, four inches long, in the center; to be seven feet long, and five and a half feet wide, and to weigh five pounds.
126. *Canvas overalls for Engineer soldiers* - of white cotton; one garment to cover the whole of the body below the waist, the breast, the shoulders, and the arms; sleeves loose, to allow a free play of the arms, with narrow wristband buttoning with one button; overalls to fasten at the neck behind with two buttons, and at the waist behind with buckle and tongue.
127. *Belts of all Enlisted Men* - black leather.
128. *Cartridge box* - according to pattern in the Ordnance Department.
129. *Drum sling* - white webbing to be provided with a brass drumstick carriage, according to pattern.
130. *Knapsack* - of painted canvas, according to pattern now issued

by the Quartermaster's Department; the great coat, when carried, to be neatly folded, not rolled, and covered by the outer flap of the knapsack.
131. *Haversack* - of painted canvas, with an inside sack unpainted, according to the pattern now issued by the Quartermaster's Department.
132. *Canteen* - of tin, covered with woolen cloth, of the pattern now issued by the Quartermaster's Department.

Paragraphs 133 through 173 omitted.

174. SPURS, (brass) - 2 spurs, 2 rowels, 2 rivets, 2 spur straps, 19 inches long, 2 roller buckles, 0.625 inch, 2 standing loops.
Length of heel for No. 1, 3½ inches; for No. 2, 3¼ inches – inside meas.
Width of heel   "   3¼   "   "   3   "
Length of shank to center of rowel, 1 inch.
Diameter of rowel, 0.85 inch.

Paragraphs 175 through 180 omitted

MILITARY STOREKEEPERS.

181. A citizen's frock coat of blue cloth, with buttons of the department to which they are attached; round black hat; pantaloons and vest, plain, white or dark blue; cravat or stock, black.

MISCELLANEOUS.

182. General Officers, and Colonels having the brevet rank of General Officers, may, on occasions of ceremony, and when not serving with troops, wear the 'dress' and 'undress' prescribed by existing regulations.
183. Officers below the grade of Colonel having brevet rank, will wear the epaulettes and shoulder straps distinctive of their army rank. In all other respects, their uniform and dress will be that of their respective regiments, corps, or departments, and according to their commissions in the same. Officers above the grade of Lieutenant Colonel by ordinary commission, having brevet rank, may wear the uniform of their respective regiments or corps, or that of General Officers, according to their brevet rank.
184. Officers are permitted to wear a plain dark blue body coat, with the button designating their respective corps, regiments, or departments, without any other mark or ornament upon it. Such a coat, however, is not to be considered as a dress for any military purpose.
185. In like manner, officers are permitted to wear a buff, white, or blue vest, with the small button of their corps, regiment, or department.
186. Officers serving with mounted troops are allowed to wear, for stable duty, a plain dark blue cloth jacket, with one or two rows of buttons down the front, according to rank; stand-up collar, sloped in front as that of the uniform coat; shoulder straps according to rank, but no other ornament.
187. The hair to be short; the beard to be worn at the pleasure of the individual; but when worn, to be kept short and neatly trimmed.
188. *A Band* will wear the uniform of the regiment or corps to which it belongs. The commanding officer may, at the expense of the corps, sanctioned by the Council of Administration, make such additions in ornaments as he may judge proper.

INDEX